Something I Remember

Book 4

Quercus Poems for Children

Poems chosen by Alan Kerr

Illustrated by Sylvia Mears

© Alan Kerr
All rights reserved

ISBN 0-9535684-5-8

Published by Quercus Publications, 8 The Barton,
Bleadon, Weston-super-Mare BS24 0AS

Printed by SP Press, Cheddar, Somerset

Contents

It was Long Ago	1
I Remember, I Remember	3
A Child of Our Time	5
One Summer Evening	6
There was a Time	7
Who?	9
What Has Happened to Lulu?	10
My Parents Kept Me from Children who were Rough	11
Small Quarrel	12
The Reverend Sabine Baring-Gould	14
maggie and milly and molly and may	16
A Bit of Colour	17
The Secret Song	18
Storm	19
Velvet Shoes	20
Snow Toward Evening	21
In the Bleak Mid-winter	22
Father, Hear the Prayer we Offer	23
The Thrush's Nest	24
Spring	25
Two Limericks	26
You Tell Me	27
Shoe, Boot! Shoe!	28
The Snare	29
Blackbird	30
Cage Bird and Sky Bird	32
The Road Not Taken	33
A Smuggler's Song	34
Time Child	37

To the Reader

Welcome to "Something I Remember". This final anthology in the Quercus Series of Poems for Children once again contains beautiful and memorable poetry for all to enjoy. The natural world, memories and childhood are some of the themes which are sensitively explored in this gleaming collection.

Well-known poets are represented here including: Eleanor Farjeon, Michael Rosen, Charles Causley and William Wordsworth. Some short biographies provide personal insights into the life and work of a number of the poets. All the poems are of the highest quality and are sure to evoke a response whether you are a young or older reader.

*When you are reading **look** for the ideas and pictures which the words convey; **listen** for the sounds of the words and their rhymes and rhythms; **feel** the joys and sadnesses, the funny and the serious things; **think about** the thoughts which have been expressed.*

I hope you enjoy the poems and gain lasting pleasure from them.

Alan Kerr

*Dedicated to my family
past and present*

It was Long Ago

I'll tell you, shall I, something I remember?
Something that still means a great deal to me.
It was long ago.

A dusty road in summer I remember,
A mountain, and an old house, and a tree
That stood, you know,

Behind the house. An old woman I remember
In a red shawl with a grey cat on her knee
Humming under a tree.

She seemed the oldest thing I can remember,
But then perhaps I was not more than three.
It was long ago.

I dragged on the dusty road, and I remember
How the old woman looked over the fence at me
And seemed to know

How it felt to be three, and called out, I remember
"Do you like bilberries and cream for tea?"
I went under the tree

And while she hummed, and the cat purred, I remember
How she filled a saucer with berries and cream for me
So long ago,

Such berries and such cream as I remember
I never had seen before, and never see
Today, you know.

And that is almost all I can remember,
The house, the mountain, the grey cat on her knee,
Her red shawl, and the tree,

And the taste of the berries, the feel of the sun I remember,
And the smell of everything that used to be
So long ago,

Till the heat on the road outside again I remember,
And how the long dusty road seemed to have for me
No end, you know.

That is the farthest thing I can remember.
It won't mean much to you. It does to me.
Then I grew up, you see.

Eleanor Farjeon

I Remember, I Remember

I remember, I remember,
The house where I was born,
The little window where the sun
Came peeping in at morn;
He never came a wink too soon,
Nor brought too long a day,
But now, I often wish the night
Had borne my breath away.

I remember, I remember,
The roses red and white,
The violets and the lily-cups,
Those flowers made of light.
The lilacs where the robin built,
And where my brother set
The laburnum on his birthday –
The tree is living yet.

I remember, I remember,
Where I was used to swing,
And thought the air must rush as fresh
To swallows on the wing;
My spirit flew in feathers then,
That is so heavy now,
The summer pools could hardly cool
The fever on my brow.

I remember, I remember,
The fir trees dark and high;
I used to think their slender tops
Were close against the sky:
It was a childish ignorance,
But now 'tis little joy
To know I'm farther off from heaven
Than when I was a boy.

                                    Thomas Hood

A Child of Our Time

I remember, I remember,
  The block where I was born,
The high-rise horror where the strain
  Left sleep and tempers torn.
Our flat was on the fourteenth floor,
  The shops were miles away,
And when the winter winds blew strong
  The whole thing seemed to sway.

I remember, I remember,
  The lifts were on the blink,
And Mum would often say, "This place
  Is driving me to drink."
There was no room to swing a cat
  And little space to grow;
I longed for neighbours when I saw
  The human ants below.

I remember, I remember,
  My father's worried frown,
The night the solid concrete cracked
  And most of it fell down.
I only hoped the architect
  Was living safe and sound,
The owner of a Georgian house
  And closer to the ground.

                              Roger Woddis

One Summer Evening
(an extract from The Prelude)

One summer evening (led by her) I found
A little boat tied to a willow tree
Within a rocky cave, its usual home.
Straight I unloosed her chain, and stepping in
Pushed from the shore. It was an act of stealth
And troubled pleasure, nor without the voice
Of mountain-echoes did my boat move on;
Leaving behind her still, on either side,
Small circles glittering idly in the moon,
Until they melted all into one track
Of sparkling light. But now, like one who rows,
Proud of his skill, to reach a chosen point
With an unswerving line, I fixed my view
Upon the summit of a craggy ridge,
The horizon's utmost boundary: for above
Was nothing but the stars and the grey sky.
She was an elfin pinnace; lustily
I dipped my oars into the silent lake,
And as I rose upon the stroke, my boat
Went heaving through the water like a swan.

— William Wordsworth

* Line 1: "her" refers to "Nature"

There was a Time
(an extract)

There was a time when meadow, grove and stream,
The earth, and every common sight,
To me did seem
Apparell'd in celestial light,
The glory and the freshness of a dream.
It is not now as it hath been of yore;
Turn wheresoe'er I may,
By night or day,
The things which I have seen I now can see no more . . .

Though nothing can bring back the hour
Of splendour in the grass, of glory in the flower;
We will grieve not, rather find
Strength in what remains behind. . .

William Wordsworth

William Wordsworth

William Wordsworth is generally recognized as one of the great English poets. His poetry includes many references to the natural world which was always a source of inspiration to him.

Born in 1770 in the Lake District William's mother died when he was seven and his father when he was thirteen. At the age of nine he was sent to the grammar school at Hawkshead, a village in the heart of rugged mountains and lakes.

During term time he lived happily with a local couple who gave him not lodgings but a real home for many years. In his epic poem, "The Prelude", from which "One Summer Evening" is taken, Wordsworth describes his school-days and his boyhood adventures exploring the local countryside. He recalls with affection the days spent walking in the autumn woods, fishing in the mountain streams, skating on a frozen lake, flying kites and galloping at great speed on horseback.

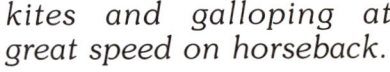

He married a childhood friend and had a family of three sons and two daughters. For most of his adult life his sister Dorothy also lived with him.

1770 – 1850

Who?

Who is that child I see wandering, wandering
Down by the side of the quivering stream?
Why does he seem not to hear, though I call to him?
Where does he come from, and what is his name?

Why do I see him at sunrise and sunset
Taking, in old-fashioned clothes, the same track?
Why, when he walks, does he cast not a shadow
Though the sun rises and falls at his back?

Why does the dust lie so thick on the hedgerow
By the great field where a horse pulls the plough?
Why do I see only meadows, where houses
Stand in a line by the riverside now?

Why does he move like a wraith by the water,
Soft as the thistledown on the breeze blown?
When I draw near him so that I may hear him,
Why does he say that his name is my own?

                                    Charles Causley

What Has Happened to Lulu?

What has happened to Lulu, mother?
  What has happened to Lu?
There's nothing in her bed but an old rag-doll
  And by its side a shoe.

Why is her window wide, mother,
  The curtain flapping free,
And only a circle on the dusty shelf
  Where her money-box used to be?

Why do you turn your head, mother,
  And why do the tear-drops fall?
And why do you crumple that note on the fire
  And say it is nothing at all?

I woke to voices late last night,
  I heard an engine roar.
Why do you tell me the things I heard
  Were a dream and nothing more?

I heard somebody cry, mother,
  In anger or in pain,
But now I ask you why, mother,
  You say it was a gust of rain.

Why do you wander about as though
  You don't know what to do?
What has happened to Lulu, mother?
  What has happened to Lu?

Charles Causley

My Parents Kept Me from Children who were Rough

My parents kept me from children who were rough
Who threw words like stones and who wore torn clothes.
Their thighs showed through rags. They ran in the street
And climbed cliffs and stripped by the country streams.

I feared more than tigers their muscles like iron
Their jerking hands and their knees tight on my arms.
I feared the salt coarse pointing of those boys
Who copied my lisp behind me on the road.

They were lithe, they sprang out behind hedges
Like dogs to bark at my world. They threw mud
While I looked the other way, pretending to smile.
I longed to forgive them, but they never smiled.

Stephen Spender

Small Quarrel

She didn't call for me as she usually does.
I shared my crisps with someone else.

I sat with someone else in assembly.
She gave me a funny look coming out.

I put a pencil mark on her maths book.
She put a felt pen mark on mine.

She moved my ruler an inch.
I moved hers a centimetre.

I just touched her PE bag with my foot.
She put the smallest tip of her tongue out.

She dipped her paint brush in my yellow.
I washed mine in her paint water.

She did something too small to tell what it was.
I *pretended* to do something.

I walked home with her as usual.
She came to my house for tea.

                              Allan Ahlberg

Allan Ahlberg

With his late wife, Janet, as the illustrator Allan Ahlberg has written many wonderful picture books and stories for young children which have become great favourites. Among the most well-known are "Each Peach Pear Plum", "Peepo", "Ten in a Bed" and the "Funnybones" series. Inventive and richly illustrated these stories will continue to enchant children and adults for years to come.

His two collections of poems about school, "Please Mrs Butler" and "Heard it in the Playground" contain feasts of poetry. Children, teachers, parents and the situations in which they find themselves are depicted in engaging, humorous, ingenious and beautifully observed poems. The scenes are familiar to everyone and each reader, young or old, will latch on to those poems which strike a particular chord.

The Reverend Sabine Baring-Gould

The Reverend Sabine Baring-Gould,
   Rector (sometime) at Lew,
Once at a Christmas party asked,
   "Whose pretty child are you?"

(The Rector's family was long,
   His memory was poor,
And as to who was who had grown
   Increasingly unsure.)

At this, the infant on the stair
   Most sorrowfully sighed.
"Whose pretty little girl am I?
   Why, *yours,* papa!" she cried.

                                   Charles Causley

The Reverend Sabine Baring-Gould (1834-1924) was Rector for 43 years at Lewtrenchard in Devon. He is the author of the hymn "Onward, Christian soldiers".

Charles Causley

Charles Causley was born in Cornwall in 1917 and has lived there for most of his life. His poems frequently refer to the places and folklore of his native county. He has published collections of poems for adults and children and was a teacher for many years. During the Second World War he served in the Royal Navy.

Charles Causley's poems contain interesting stories, lots of people and plenty of humour. They are beautifully crafted and run with flowing rhythm and rhyme. The poetry is very readable but it also contains much wisdom which is well worth reflecting upon.

maggie and milly and molly and may

maggie and milly and molly and may
went down to the beach (to play one day)

and maggie discovered a shell that sang
so sweetly she couldn't remember her troubles, and

milly befriended a stranded star
whose rays five languid fingers were;

and molly was chased by a horrible thing
which raced sideways while blowing bubbles: and

may came home with a smooth round stone
as small as a world and as large as alone.

For whatever we lose (like a you or a me)
it's always ourselves we find in the sea

E E Cummings

A Bit of Colour

Grey was the morn, all things were grey,
   'Twas winter more than spring;
A bleak east wind swept o'er the land,
   And sobered everything.

Grey was the sky, the fields were grey,
   The hills, the woods, the trees –
Distance and foreground – all the scene
   Was grey in the grey breeze.

Grey cushions, and a grey skin rug,
   A dark grey wicker trap,
Grey were the ladies' hats and cloaks,
   And grey my coat and cap.

A narrow, lonely, grey old lane;
   And lo, on a grey gate,
Just by the side of a grey wood,
   A sooty sweep there sat!

With grimy chin 'twixt grimy hands
   He sat and whistled shrill;
And in his sooty cap he wore
   A yellow daffodil.

And often when the days are dull,
   I seem to see him still –
The jaunty air, the sooty face –
   And the yellow daffodil.

Horace Smith

The Secret Song

Who saw the petals
  drop from the rose?
I, said the spider,
But nobody knows.

Who saw the sunset
  flash on a bird?
I, said the fish,
But nobody heard.

Who saw the fog
  come over the sea?
I, said the sea pigeon,
Only me.

Who saw the first
  green light of the sun?
I, said the night owl,
The only one.

Who saw the moss
  creep over the stone?
I, said the grey fox,
All alone.

Margaret Wise Brown

Storm

They're at it again
the wind and the rain
It all started
when the wind
took the window
by the collar
and shook it
with all its might
Then the rain
butted in
What a din
they'll be at it all night
Serves them right
if they go home in the morning
and the sky won't let them in

                                        Roger McGough

Velvet Shoes

Let us walk in the white snow
  In a soundless space;
With footsteps quiet and slow,
  At a tranquil pace,
  Under veils of white lace.

I shall go shod in silk,
  And you in wool,
White as a white cow's milk,
  More beautiful
  Than the breast of a gull.

We shall walk through the still town
  In a windless peace;
We shall step upon white down,
  Upon silver fleece,
  Upon softer than these.

We shall walk in velvet shoes:
  Wherever we go
Silence will fall like dews
  On white silence below.
  We shall walk in the snow.

                    Elinor Wylie

Snow Toward Evening

Suddenly the sky turned grey.
The day
which had been bitter and chill,
grew soft and still.
Quietly
from some invisible blossoming tree
millions of petals cool and white
drifted and blew,
lifted and flew,
fell with the falling night.

                                        Melville Cane

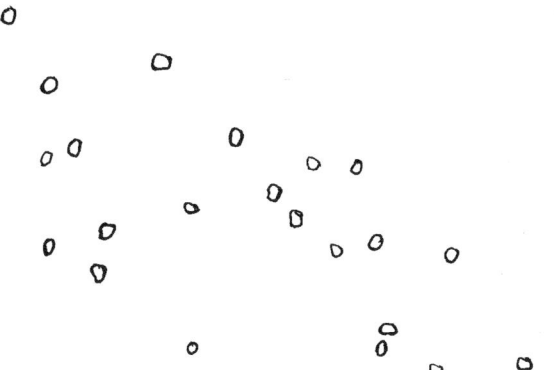

In the Bleak Mid-winter

In the bleak mid-winter
  Frosty wind made moan,
Earth stood hard as iron,
  Water like a stone;
Snow had fallen, snow on snow,
  Snow on snow,
In the bleak mid-winter,
  Long ago.

Our God, heaven cannot hold him
  Nor earth sustain;
Heaven and earth shall flee away
  When he comes to reign;
In the bleak mid-winter
  A stable-place sufficed
The Lord God Almighty,
  Jesus Christ.

What can I give him,
  Poor as I am?
If I were a shepherd
  I would bring a lamb;
If I were a wise man
  I would do my part;
Yet what I can I give him –
  Give my heart.

Christina Rossetti

Father, Hear the Prayer we Offer

Father, hear the prayer we offer;
Not for ease that prayer shall be,
But for strength that we may ever
Live our lives courageously.

Not for ever in green pastures
Do we ask our way to be;
But the steep and rugged pathway
May we tread rejoicingly.

Not for ever by still waters
Would we idly rest and stay;
But would smite the living fountains
From the rocks along our way.

Be our strength in hours of weakness,
In our wanderings be our guide;
Through endeavour, failure, danger,
Father, be thou at our side.

L M Willis

The Thrush's Nest

Within a thick and spreading hawthorn bush,
That overhung a molehill large and round,
I heard from morn to morn a merry thrush
Sing hymns to sunrise, and I drank the sound
With joy, and oft – an intruding guest,
I watched her secret toils from day to day;
How true she warped the moss to form her nest,
And modelled it within with wood and clay.
And by and by, like heath-bells gilt with dew,
There lay her shining eggs as bright as flowers,
Ink-spotted-over, shells of greeny blue:
And there I witnessed in the summer hours
A brood of Nature's minstrels chirp and fly,
Glad as the sunshine and the laughing sky.

John Clare

Spring

Nothing is so beautiful as spring –
When weeds, in wheels, shoot long and lovely and lush;
Thrush's eggs look little low heavens, and thrush
Through the echoing timber does so rinse and wring
The ear, it strikes like lightning to hear him sing;
The glassy peartree leaves and blooms, they brush
The descending blue; that blue is all in a rush
With richness; the racing lambs too have fair their fling.

What is all this juice and all this joy?
A strain of the earth's sweet being in the beginning
In Eden garden. – Have, get, before it cloy,
Before it cloud, Christ, lord, and sour with sinning,
Innocent mind and Mayday in girl and boy,
Most, O maid's child, thy choice and worthy the winning.

Gerard Manley Hopkins

Two Limericks

There was a Young Girl of Majorca,
Whose aunt was a very fast walker;
She walked seventy miles
And leaped fifteen stiles
Which astonished that Girl of Majorca.

* * * * * *

There was a young lady of Diss
Who thought skating was absolute bliss
Till love turned to hate
When a slip of her skate
siɥʇ ǝʞᴉl ƃuᴉɥʇǝɯos dn ɥsᴉuᴉɟ ɹǝɥ ǝpɐɯ

You Tell Me

Here are the football results:
League Division Fun
Manchester United won, Manchester City lost.
Crystal Palace 2, Buckingham Palace 1
Millwall Leeds nowhere
Wolves 8 A cheese roll and had a cup of tea 2
Aldershot 3 Buffalo Bill shot 2
Evertonill, Liverpool's not very well either
Newcastle's Heaven Sunderland's a very nice place 2
Ipswhich one? You tell me.

Michael Rosen

Shoe, Boot! Shoe!

Dear Shoe, I've got
a crush on you,
I think you're
b-o-o-t-i-f-u-l.
Please, could you take a
shine to me or do you find me dull?
Dear Boot, you are a silly clog so kindly hold your tongue.
You are a heel and my soft soul, by you, will not be won.
Boot felt his throat tie in a knot.   Shoe'd walked all over him!
And   now   he's   stashed   back   on   the   shelf,
alone,   *out on a limb.*

Gina Douthwaite

The Snare

I hear a sudden cry of pain
   There is a rabbit in a snare:
Now I hear the cry again,
   But I cannot tell from where.

But I cannot tell from where
   He is calling out for aid;
Crying on the frightened air,
   Making everything afraid.

Making everything afraid,
   Wrinkling up his little face,
As he cries again for aid;
   And I cannot find the place.

And I cannot find the place
   Where his paw is in the snare:
Little one, Oh, little one,
   I am searching everywhere.

James Stephens

Blackbird

My wife saw it first –
I was reading the evening paper.
Come and look, she said.

It was trying to drink
Where water had formed on a drain-cover.
It was shabby with dying.
It did not move until I was very close –
Then hopped off, heavily,
Disturbing dead leaves.

We left water, crumbs,
It did not touch them
But waited among the leaves,
Silently.

This morning was beautiful:
Sunlight, other birds
Singing.

It was outside the door.
I picked it up
And it was like holding feathered air.
I wrapped what was left

Incongruously
In green sycamore leaves
And buried it near the tree,
Inches down.

This evening
I find it difficult to concentrate
On the paper, the news
Of another cosmonaut.

                                        Christopher Leach

Cage Bird and Sky Bird

Cage Bird swung
From an apple tree
And his cage was of silver
And ivory.
  Nobody can be so happy, so happy;
    Sang the Cage Bird.

Sky Bird sang
From a cloudless sky
And his wings were wide
And bright his eye.
  Nobody can be as happy as I;
    Sang the Sky Bird.

That wild song
To the garden fell
And Cage Bird heard it, in
His silver cell.
  Are you free then, are you truly free?
    Cried the Cage Bird.

Sky Bird flew
In the trail of the sun
And swiftly he soared, away
From the garden.
  Sadly sang Cage Bird, when the day was done;
    Sang the Cage Bird.

Leslie Norris

The Road Not Taken

Two roads diverged in a yellow wood,
And sorry I could not travel both
And be one traveller, long I stood
And looked down one as far as I could
To where it bent in the undergrowth;

Then took the other, as just as fair,
And having perhaps the better claim,
Because it was grassy and wanted wear;
Though as for that the passing there
Had worn them really about the same,

And both that morning equally lay
In leaves no step had trodden black.
Oh, I kept the first for another day!
Yet knowing how way leads on to way,
I doubted if I should ever come back.

I shall be telling this with a sigh
Somewhere ages and ages hence:
Two roads diverged in a wood, and I –
I took the one less travelled by,
And that has made all the difference.

Robert Frost

A Smuggler's Song

If you wake at midnight and hear a horse's feet,
Don't go drawing back the blind, or looking in the street,
Them that asks no questions isn't told a lie.
Watch the wall, my darling, while the Gentlemen go by!
   Five and twenty ponies,
   Trotting through the dark –
   Brandy for the Parson,
   Baccy for the Clerk;
   Laces for a lady, letters for a spy;
And watch the wall, my darling, while the Gentlemen go by!

Running round the woodlump if you chance to find
Little barrels, roped and tarred, all full of brandy-wine,
Don't you shout to come and look, nor use 'em for your play.
Put the brushwood back again - and they'll be gone next day!

If you see the stable-door setting open wide;
If you see a tired horse lying down inside;
If your mother mends a coat cut about and tore;
If the lining's wet and warm – don't you ask no more!

If you meet King George's men, dressed in blue and red,
You be careful what you say, and mindful what is said.
If they call you "pretty maid", and chuck you 'neath the chin,
Don't you tell where no one is, nor yet where no one's been!

Knocks and footsteps round the house – whistles after dark –
You've no call for running out till the housedogs bark.
Trusty's here and Pincher's here, and see how dumb they lie –
They don't fret to follow when the Gentlemen go by!

If you do as you've been told, likely there's a chance,
You'll be give a dainty doll, all the way from France,
With a cap of Valenciennes, and a velvet hood –
A present from the Gentlemen, along o' being good!
    Five and twenty ponies,
    Trotting through the dark –
    Brandy for the Parson,
    Baccy for the Clerk.
Them that asks no questions isn't told a lie –
Watch the wall, my darling, while the Gentlemen go by!

Rudyard Kipling

Rudyard Kipling

Rudyard Kipling was born in India in 1865 but was taken to England with his younger sister at the age of six. Here he spent an unhappy childhood, believing that he had been deserted by his parents. For more than five years he endured beatings and solitary confinements at the hands of his foster parents while he stayed with them at what he called the "House of Desolation".

Later on he attended a boarding school in North Devon where he had a passion for English literature and became the editor of the school paper.

When he was seventeen he returned to India to work as a journalist and he also began to write poems and short stories. He became a serious writer and eventually settled down to live in England. In 1907 he received the Nobel Prize for Literature.

The story for which he is best known is "The Jungle Book" and many people are familiar with his "Just So Stories" which include "How the Camel got his Hump" and "How the Leopard got his Spots".

1865 - 1936

Time Child

Dandelion, dandelion,
Dandelion flower,
If I breathe upon thee
Pray tell me the hour.

Little child, little child,
Little child I pray,
Breathe but gently on me
Lest you blow the time away.

                               Gareth Owen

Acknowledgements

Grateful thanks are due to the following for permission to use copyright material:

David Higham Associates for **It was Long Ago** by Eleanor Farjeon from *Silver Sand and Snow,* Michael Joseph; for **Who?** by Charles Causley from *Collected Poems 1951 – 2000,* Macmillan; for **What Has Happened to Lulu?** and **The Reverend Sabine Baring-Gould** by Charles Causley from *Selected Poems for Children,* Macmillan; the New Statesman for **A Child of Our Time** by Roger Woddis © New Statesman, 1998; Ed Victor Limited for **My Parents Kept Me from Children who were Rough** by Stephen Spender; Penguin Books Limited for **Small Quarrel** by Allan Ahlberg from *Please Mrs Butler*, Kestrel 1983, © Allan Ahlberg; and also for **You Tell Me** by Michael Rosen from *You Tell Me* by Roger McGough and Michael Rosen, Kestrel 1979, © Michael Rosen, 1979; W W Norton and Company Limited for **maggie and milly and molly and may** by E E Cummings reprinted from *Complete Poems 1904 – 1962* by E E Cummings edited by George J Firmage © 1991 by the Trustees for the E E Cummings Trust and George James Firmage; PFD on behalf of Roger McGough for **Storm** by Roger McGough © Roger McGough; Harcourt Inc for **Snow Toward Evening** from *January Garden* by Melville Cane, © 1926 by Harcourt Inc and renewed 1954 by Melville Cane; the Random House Group Limited for **Shoe, Boot! Shoe!** by Gina Douthwaite from *Picture a Poem* by Gina Douthwaite, Hutchinson/Red Fox; and also for **The Road Not Taken** by Robert Frost from *The Poetry of Robert Frost* edited by Edward Connery Lathem, Jonathan Cape; the Society of Authors as the Literary Representative of the estate of James Stephens for **The Snare** by James Stephens; Leslie Norris for his poem **Cage Bird and**

Sky Bird; A P Watt Limited on behalf of The National Trust for Places of Historic Interest or Natural Beauty for **A Smuggler's Song** by Rudyard Kipling; HarperCollins Publishers Limited for **Time Child** by Gareth Owen from *Salford Road*, Kestrel Books.

For the two portraits, grateful thanks are due also to:

"Dove Cottage, The Wordsworth Trust" for permission to reproduce the portrait of **William Wordsworth** by Henry Edridge, 1806; the Kipling Society for the portrait of **Rudyard Kipling**.

Every effort has been made to obtain permission to reproduce copyright material. The publisher apologizes, however, for any copyright which has not been acknowledged and will be pleased to rectify this in any future edition.